Now and Then

poems by

Pete Gage

THE HOBNOB PRESS
2023

First published in the United Kingdom in 2023

by The Hobnob Press,
8 Lock Warehouse, Severn Road, Gloucester GL1 2GA
www.hobnobpress.co.uk

© Pete Gage 2023

The Author hereby asserts his moral rights to be identified as the Author of the Work.

All rights reserved. No part of this publication may be reproduced, stored in a retrieval system, or transmitted in any form or by any means, electronic, mechanical, photocopying, recording or otherwise, without the prior permission of the publisher and copyright holder.

British Library Cataloguing in Publication Data
A catalogue record for this book is available from the British Library

ISBN 978-1-914407-53-6

Typeset in Adobe Garamond Pro 14/17 pt.
Typesetting and origination by John Chandler

Cover Art:
'Conductor and Renaissance Musicians'
by David H. Evans 1929 – 1988

Dedication
*This selection of my early and recent poems
is compiled in affectionate memory of,
and gratitude to, Crysse Morrison (1944 – 2022),
whose inspiration and care encouraged me
to re-kindle my love of poetry.*

There Beneath Your Hair (1968)   7
What Praise (1969)   8
Before Such Silence As Love Procures Began (1969) 10
Sudden Death (1969)   11
What Child There Ever Was So Sweet (1969)   12
Small Simple Lot I Ask (1969)   13
Junes (1971)   15
Simple Was (1971)   16
Whenever The Baby (1972)   17
Some Flower Inside Me (1975)   18
Poem To Lesley (1977)   19
Novel (1977)   20
Quietly Speaking (1982)   22
If My Eyes Were Clear To See With (2017)   24
The Lie (2021)   26
Choices (2021)   27

I Walk As If Preparing (2022)	28
Fantasy (2022)	30
The Seeds (2022)	31
Unconscious Neglect (2021)	32
Shingle And Sand (2022)	34
Death Of Fear (2022)	35
These Pages Turned (2022)	37
All Things Equal (2022)	38
Far Flung Corners (2022)	40
Finding In Others (2022)	41
Silent Beginnings (2022)	43
Thought (2022)	45
Still Water (2022)	47
May Morning (2022)	49
Last Train (2022)	51
Requiem Æternam (2022)	53
Dona Eis Requiem (2022)	55
Birth Day (2022)	56
Mutual Demise (2022)	57
Chameleon (2022)	58
Magnificent Day (2022)	60
Storm Nor Stress (2022)	62
The Blackbird (2022)	63
Off The Radar (2022)	65
Warlords (2022)	67
Past, Present, Future (2022)	69
My Hero, Ellie (2022)	70
Ode To Poetry (2022)	71
Homecoming (2022)	73

Cotton Sheets (2022)	75
Perhaps (2022)	76
Unknown Depths (for Tristan) (2022)	78
Essence (2022)	80
Solo (2022)	81
Love No more (2022)	82
Only This (2022)	84
Tanker (2022)	85
D.H.E. (2022)	86
Three for Crysse (2022)	87
Now And Then (2022)	90
For Lizzi (2022)	91
Where? (2023)	92
Oblivious (2023)	93
Each To The Other (2023)	94
Untold Mystery (2023)	95
You In The Mirror (2023)	96

There Beneath Your Hair

There beneath your hair
that spared, scant-clad,
your thoughts inside your head,
lies one
for whom my search is dead.

There, behind your fiery eyes,
beneath your wise
or rippled brow with sleep
it lies,
and never will be read.

What Praise

What praise would I give for the pounding waves
on rocks now washed by salty tears?
And what for the grains of virgin sand
that make a home for a crab?

What could I give to the hill-high sheep,
or the galloping riderless horse?
What praise for the silent white-rim cliffs
guarding gulls and their nests on high.

With what would I gaze at the craning blades
full with the sap of summer turf?
With what at the weeping willow tree,
its weary arms and thick-veined leaves.

O what would I hear in the air and the wind
round clouds that breathe in time with me
as I stand upon these hills of pine
looking down on the sea at dawn?

What would I do but offer a leaf
to a random snail on a garden path?
What would I do but what I do now?
Sad little but what I say.

To these and all the natural things
upon this burning land, I'd give

but all I can, but ah, I lie in London's bed
til the summer runs me dry.

Before Such Silence as Love Procures Began

Before such silence as love procures began, when
first your hand had touched my heart . . .
before your words could no more describe my kiss
than the heat of the lull describes the storm . . .
before the moon and sun knew neither night
nor day of ours who day and night would love . . .
before those times, there passed no time
but the time it took for the thunder's flash,
that spark that smashed to tears of light
now doused in the puddles of forgotten dreams.

Now, such silence as that has ceased;
no rapture holds the memory
of love's quick-changing course.
Love was prepared in silence;
now we sing its thundering crescendo.

Sudden Death

I live in fear of sudden death;
what measures short-lived love?
I live in fear of losing what
the time it took to kiss could kill;
the love that was a life until
the fear of sudden death.

I live in fear of losing life;
what might have cut it short?
I live in fear of losing what
had governed how I try to live.
All that time could ever give,
it takes with sudden death.

What Child There Ever Was So Sweet As This

What child there ever was so sweet as this,
was a child more chaste
than a child in a mother's womb;
and there is no child for me more pure
than she whose mother laid soft a kiss
upon my half-closed eyes one day
like it were a dream from which i'd woken;
eyelids cleansed of all their sleep,
til I saw, and felt, and found
all of life was clean.
What child there ever was so sweet as this,
that lay unblemished in my lover's womb,
breathing only of my lover's breath,
feeling only of my lover's heart,
was surely more than child to me,
was reason so to live.

Small Simple Lot I Ask

Small simple lot I ask;
no winging flight through life.
No memory of bad old days,
just simple ways of life.
No golden chalice from which to drink,
no marble floor on which to walk.
I have but small enough a lot
as now; there's not much more I ask.

Small and simple lot I need;
not ask, but need for heaven's sake.
Send no guardian angel,
for my angel has arrived.
There is no wealth I crave or need;
humanity is all from those who were inhuman,
to bestow what I implore.

Small simple lot I ask;
small measure for a life from which
will ooze the sap for many later lives to sup.
Measure me by simplicity,
count my mellow tones.
Sprinkle humane fertility
by speaking of all I own.
All I own is beautiful;
small simple lot's the more
than now the child within me desires.

What is there more?
A season of love, a blooming of a bud.
Do we, in this Spring and blossoming of life,
stand no chance so late in this,
the wintering of our earth?

Junes

Junes were once when truth was soft
on bleeding beads of brows of ours;
once they were months that forced our hearts
through pores as clogged as dust can do.

Junes would cleanse in the season's height;
summer rain, through haze and blossom,
when the soul would feed on fertile soil,
hungry for the warmth of a summer sun.

June it was first planted seeds
from which we nurtured our sometime peace;
ah, June, unblemished, simple days,
once our fragrant life's reward.

Now, as June caresses other hearts
like mine that savoured all its juice,
I can only feel the thump of life.
As time takes speed and spins me on,
there's a potent majesty in the wideness of reality,
the gaping chasms that the rest of life must fill.

Would that Junes were Junes again
as first when I would feel their joy.
There's no month such that saves the failing
grace of the moaning year.

Simple

Simple was, that
sadly, truth evades;
whatever could,
is what we could not save.

And when that simple was,
the same was too soon kissed;
whatever simple was,
is what we've so long missed.

But soon the truth reveals it;
the honesty turns pure;
our wisdom keeps the seed of it,
and simple stays secure.

Whenever the Baby

Whenever the baby,
wet as the woman,
white as the blue-white
flesh of its temple,
kicks at the silence
for hell and its sickness,
a reason less shallow
than ours to continue
with reason, is come to the fore.

And however the gentleman,
standing as guardian,
baffles his way round
the paths of his having to,
he will not say no to
the entrance of children
bearing on a bib
their reason for being;
he will merely let enter the more.

Some Flower Inside Me

Some flower inside me
sees the time of day;
some day inside me starts the rest of life;
some life inside me
tells me who I am;
that the seed inside the flower feeds a dream.

Some dream inside me
throws a meaning forth;
some meaning took a soul the time to grow;
some growth inside me
makes the heart I hold
a rock on which I finally can live.

If to be the lover of this life,
then flower inside will feed my dream;
and if to be whose dream is of the soul,
then living is the meaning for my heart.

Some past inside me
asks to be set free;
some freedom in me opens up the door;
some door inside me
opens up to life,
that I may live as now I find I do.

Poem to Lesley

Last lady,
not the laughing lady at me,
smiling at the gate;
how the sweetness of you
stills a stirring fate.

Soft lady,
once a time had you lost,
stumbling in the trap;
how the simpleness of your love
fills the found man's gap.

Last lady,
how the sweetness of your love
stills echoes in my dream,
peace that he's been seeking all his life,
he who holds you high in his esteem.

Novel

My need has become desire;
sharp-toothed and hard of hearing,
I rage on, relentlesssly certain
that I should have left my youth
at the front gate
and leaned with strong hands
on the solid walls inside.

But a demon in the soul,
thought in a clear mind,
or maggot in my fruitfulness,
lures me to a self-deception
only felt by those I've seen
sometimes in public houses,
whiskey glass in hand all evening,
and heart in mouth all day.

I have lured and it is gone.
I have serenity and stability at my feet.
From this seat I feel a need,
in my comfort, to reflect.

My need has become desire;
and I am plagued again, without fever;
touched without pain
by a child in me

that sings and always will;
I will always sing.

Quietly Speaking

Quietly speaking, just supposing,
far from a mother's training,
the smallest part of these nonsenses,
and all the futile reasons for it, lost in a stifled cry;
who now, to model, next to follow?

Neatly governed, where to tread?
Masking all that went before us,
smartly packaged, then discarded;
not to hear it in the dreaming,
as it infiltrates the memory,
turning up on other doorsteps,
who are we to interfere?

Contravening man-made orders,
with mostly not a moment's rest.
First blood, all that's empty, close to the edge;
under which leadership,
all things equal, finding refuge
having taken time to simmer.
Not so able on the journey
making most of comprehending,
drawing out the bloody sabre.

Was it worth it? Who was counting?
And what difference under fire?
Here we are, closely watching

words unfolding in relenting moments,
mentioning because we need to,
to understand the why or wherefore.

More a habit or compulsion; not a real motivation;
more a measure of condition, how it is, or meant to be.
Being equal, all things gently, can we ever comprehend?
Fellowship in man's dilemma, smiling dangerously,
we have walked a thousand walkways,
undeterred by reality.

If My Eyes Were Clear To See With

If my eyes were clear to see with,
then surely they would know
how my tears conspire to cloud them,
untruths distort their view.
But present is how I've come to be
though now will soon be past,
decaying all sense of time endured.
I'd seek a reason for this blindness,
if I didn't already know.

If my heart were more than muscle,
most surely it would ache
with my dead-weight body down below;
that moves, yet cannot feel;
that stirs though only flesh surviving,
or bones shuddering in their gristle,
their water daring the skin to quake,
cool on the dry surface of my being.
This body no longer feeds like it did;
its sinews contract without compassion.
I'd seek a reason for it to die
if I didn't already know.

I cower in secret, from a darkened corner,
hiding both the stirrings of my fear;
fear that drove me clambering on my journey.
Living by these rules I learned

to side-step all their trappings
to avoid their consuming animal,
and to use them as my muse.
But now I count the passing seconds
aimlessly awaiting transformation,
peering into dark old caves
of mouldy walls and holy sinners,
not knowing quite just when it will come.
I'd seek a reason for this degeneration
if I didn't already know.

The Lie

Swallow hard to keep the lie from spilling;
clench your teeth upon white knuckles,
wide-eyed fear in your glances;
you are waiting for the axe to fall.
Who decides to break the chains,
unlock the rage within,
to witness the first drops of rain
upon your dried up ruins?

Hold fast the moment of perception
until its bliss is spent
and the fading memory has been embraced.
The fire in the belly,
driving you on to victorious truth.
Your race cannot be won,
all your victims will be swallowed with the lie.

Choices

Tempted by the chances
that surround me,
I take the route
less likely to succeed.
Choices
depending on my own circumstance.
Like karma they never
stand alone in their own light.
Truth looms
where suddenly the breath is still;
without the movement of breath,
l choose to enter, where
silence now prevails.
Let silence caress
where flesh
and idle thought dissolve,
knowing only this:
words are but embellishment;
and truth lies
beyond its own
description.

I Walk As If Preparing

I walk as if preparing,
as if upon my guard I step
in time to the slow beating
of an ever fleeting dream I have
on a whim that I may one day rue.

I stand alone preparing,
as I discard the memories kept
inside this shell of a man I used to be,
whose strength is sapped;
my dignity denies a last goodbye.

I wander through the castles I have built
on the edges of a distant cliff I used to climb,
unperturbed by dangers there,
then being not the day to die.
I challenge the gods I dealt with,
defending all that's worthy in me,
as the warrior within
breaks out in victorious song.
But cautiously I tread,
with steady hand held high,
in recognition of mistakes I made before
this heavenly age had blessed me.

I walk as if preparing
to awaken from this hazy dreamscape

to the eternal bliss of my waiting immortality.
Blessed by the memory of yesterday;
now at peace, where hope is sprung
in the pleasant meadows of tomorrow;
hope scooped up in sorrowful times
of forgotten harmony or distant heartache.
There never was a sorrow quite like this;
tears are yet to fall in the quietness of a whisper;
it is their last broken moment.

Fantasy

I thought of you as family:
you, so recently real to me;
you, who touched my heart;
you, whom I no longer see, nor give to.

You remind me of the one I left behind;
she has been long gone.
Not like now, you, suddenly;
vanished from my life;
all tidily wrapped up, not a stone unturned.
You walked with a feminine swagger,
a nonchalance she had when her mood was high;
your eyes were green like hers;
and grey in a sombre light.
Her hair was short,
to reveal her face
with a smile so much like your's.
And as I held your hand as once I did with her,
I wondered was it real,
or was it all just fantasy?

The Seeds

When you ask how the seeds I sow
might grow inside my garden,
words do not take root.
Nor can the heart translate.
There are always seeds inside
whose path is yet unchosen.

Now as I lie, motionless before sleep,
it is only the soul that moves across the page.
It wants to speak, naked and raw,
unguided by thought, born without notion.

These seeds are wisps of thought,
born of the heart, unopened
by speech or poem; seeds planted in
the soil of the unconscious,
nurtured by reason in the night.
They are not mine.
I just follow behind them,
tidying my garden:
my poem in the leaves.

Unconscious Neglect

They desert you in the end;
the old man sat reflecting.
Desertion by way of unconscious neglect.
Aware of his own misdemeanors of the past,
friendships he had tired of;
aware of having hurt or abandoned them,
family or loved ones now gone.

There are few acquaintances now;
some in the town, some in the cafes;
a few at a distance;
but most of whom he can no longer trust,
or gush forth as once he did,
with emotion or wild expression
and no fear of reprisal.

This, the right time for reflection;
another chapter in a full life.
A full life amounting merely
to things achieved, or experienced;
not the fulness that comes
from an inner light that shines
beyond this bland reality.

Is it time to discount such
achievements and gains as superfluous,
this change in me playing a part for others

now unable to relate?
Were they only interested
in revelling in this local fame,
unknowingly chaining me to the past?
Unconscious conditional friendship:
unconscious neglect?

Shingle and Sand

I look to find her gone once more,
in the ever-changing shore-line;
her face in the foam
as it dissipates with sighs
over shingle and sand.

The sun glistens on distant peaks
in the ebb and flow of endless tides.
I swim to the rhythm of my own breath,
each stroke in time
with a memory.

Our land lies up ahead,
our old refuge and solace
from aching hearts and limbs.
But now my belly slides and scrapes
over jagged sea-bed shells
where once a soft, low-tide would caress.
She was my all-encompassing sea.

Death of Fear

Losing faith in gathering crowds,
learning not to show your hand;
sudden noises make you nervous;
drifting on a sea of sand.

Breaking out in sweat you relish,
aching limbs from climbing hills,
begging unknown gods to save you,
killing the root of all your ills.

Should you turn to face the demon,
flaking as your legs now falter,
or should you look for sanctuary
inside a nearby church or altar?

Never has the land subsided
where you stand, as now it does,
you are sinking; rising tides
now wash away the land that was.

For this catastrophe has led you
to new places in your head;
you have fought and you have struggled;
now you find that fear is dead.

The breaking down of all life's patterns
brings benefit as well as trial;

the just rewards bring meaning to you,
eliminating self-denial.

These Pages Turned

These pages turned reveal no word
of pain or malice I may feel
for circumstances here recalled,
or roads I stumbled down before.

A new voice. cleansing all that rises from within,
young, that once would burn my throat till raw,
replenishes the soil of these earthly ramblings,
declaring holy truths I utter now.

No sign of strain or struggle taunts me
as I lean towards the sun,
unafraid of dying as I might have been before,
welcoming the freedom in my death.

Commonplace and uninspiring
though my words were once before,
my heart at last receives these garlands;
is it my reason or my madness you adore?

As witness to this holy conversion,
I reach to turn the fertile ground,
no longer wary of disbelievers;
my children lead the way.

All Things Equal

Forever though I dream,
never has a dream portrayed a truth
so clear as this that sings to me
among these waking hours.
Guilt and sorrow summon the word,
their source lies in the gut
of universal experience.
From deep within the centuries,
the poem passes through me;
not born within, neither mine to claim;
nor of painter I may have loved,
for he lies dead, only remembered
as a muse I summoned to open doors
for a poet's eloquence.
With voice of depth and sweetness,
sprung from the wells of youth and the aged,
this the teacher lies down with the pupil,
and the song, with its tune and its lyric.
Truth was never ours to give;
Its word is only passing through;
a connection that links our inner core,
 your's to mine, Self to Self
in the magisterial symbiosis
of one to the next,
one to the other.
Within begets without, all things equal,
the thread unbroken that weaves a coat

for the shepherd in the morning light,
or a shawl for the grieving widow,
all things equal, all things one.

Far-flung Corners

We walked the land
before the ground was dry,
the blossom fell to cover
where our shadows used to lie.

They will not return, those lovers;
this grief is part of the love they shared.

They weep in far-flung corners,
unhearing and unheard,
bodies growing old
with hearts of sorrow,
filled with only yesterday.

Finding in Others

I found in some,
a shallow grave;
those who died
before their song was sung.
There was little here
to right the wrong
or show the way,
their road was blocked
by experience,
accumulated power
along a not so sacred path.
The spirit writhed
within them
but their chosen way
held fast,
clouding all hope
of reprieve.

I found in others
a common thread,
rare amongst the lost;
I thought we were as one.
We'd stand as if
reflected there;
our core within,
depth unknown,
and not without a touch

of simplicity.
We spoke of steps
that lead us to the well.

With suffering as our metaphor,
the urge to share
so much more
than all our worldly
thoughts exchanged.
We held instead our outstretched hand,
pure as at our first communion.

Silent Beginnings

You sat serene
in your child's garden,
your calm demeanor
cool on my wind-swept brow;
my heart was hastening
to its new-found rhythm.
Your distant gaze
effortlessly seduced
the angels into believing
it was I who had caused
wild flowers to smother the earth,
so moist beneath
their shimmering canopy.

You were
the jewel on my horizon,
the marker with which
we found exquisite alchemy.
If to enter was to err,
then I had wandered
far from home,
pursued by grief
that I wore like a glove
with such a natural ease.
At the finish-line I fell,
your kiss so soft
fell hard upon my cheek,

my head still spinning
on your fertile meadows.

You look upon me now
with a look of quiet disdain
I could have once predicted.
All that we endured
passes like a funeral
through our corridors,
from our silent beginnings
to this, our solitary end.

Thought

Thought haunts the aching soul;
it sidles in un-noticed,
grumbling out its mono-tones
to the tune of ancient memory,
its merciless distractions,
witnessing the victims' demise
and littering the purity
with melancholic awakenings.

Thought leaves us lost
in its vice-like grip,
oblivious to a blackbird song,
or suspicious of a stranger's glance.
Lost in its persistent ramblings
we stumble over the ruins
of our hungry pasts:
love and loss, fragments of delight;
voices of the self,
all complicating the present
with unconscious deliberation.

Thought heralds
the ghosts of past realities,
imaginary griefs
conjured within
for our own perusal
as we make our way

to a poem's first breath,
not recognizing the soul within.

Thought is always old;
it disturbs the peace of being,
infiltrating our sorrow,
meddling with our truth
and haunting the aching soul.

Still Water

Journey's end or stepping stone,
you've travelled many a road;
familiar stories on your own;
your troubles you unload.

Still water is the leveller;
you meditate on this;
once you were the reveler;
nothing you would miss.

Communal re-connection,
will you take another chance?
You might not find perfection
but with spirits you will dance.

You watch with such compassion;
it's how you've lived till now,
master in your fashion
of what the senses will allow.

Beginnings are not over;
endings not yet here;
you wandered as a rover,
travelled with no fear.

You arranged your words like flowers;
chose how they should fall;

if they lasted only minutes
there was beauty to recall.

And as the night grows clearer
watch out for idle thought;
hold stillness all the nearer,
let go of all you sought.

May Morning

Rain fell in the night
leaving the air moist and warm.
A dove is cooing to the rhythm of the breeze.
The two maple trees are singing
like waves coming in on a distant shore-line.

A low-toned response from a second dove
brings unplanned harmony
composed in a moment of conception
and carried through the air
around the small garden.
The grass emits
the fragrance that comes
after the first mowing.

All is peaceful and fresh,
with a sense of new beginnings.
Tomato plants have taken root
like baby chicks reaching skyward,
alert and strong.
Sweet pea and dahlia, jasmine,
holly-hock and English rose
are alive in their mid-May dance.

The air feels clear and clean,
every sound, natural.
There is nothing troubling the senses,

content and alone with my fresh coffee,
my notebook and my pen.
Here comes some gentle rain!
Welcome!

Last Train

When the last train pulls out
there'll be no guard on board.
Straight to the end of the line
with no stops on the way;
no jumping off to make amends
to those who wave goodbye.
They'll stand upon their platforms
searching with puzzled expression
for one more chance to forgive
the mistakes of a distant past.
Darting eyes, hypnotized
by blurred visions of empty carriages;
all but one, with a face that tells
the whole story of this final journey.

There'll be no time for laughter
as the wheels go rattling round.
There'll be no room for tears
save for the chronic interventions
in hysterical chantings
of those who don't ask why,
life still passing them by.
No space for reflection
or quiet explanations
above the rhythm's
relentless pulse.

Decreasing demands,
before the final furlong,
to answer for being,
or reason, or seeing.
Terminal looming,
releasing the burden,
imminent freedom:
the unattended journey's end.

Requiem Æternam

Reflections in each the others' eyes
dissolve as melted wax,
distorted beyond the belief
that this would be
the last subsiding chapter
in a life that breathes no more.

The last nail in the casket
secured the the final blow;
time and tired scenarios
tarnished our shining armour.
Submissive pleas for a reprieve
from the relentless bid
to attain clarity
amidst our chaotic passions,
have receded into the silence
of our ever-diminishing returns.

Bonds of friendship hang loose,
reduced to threadbare stitches
in the fading tapestry of our story.
We exchange but nodding glances
as if to an old acquaintance.
All that's left is to gather
the remnants of our fallen garments,
salvaging the strands

of old memories while we can,
before the last of our tears have dried.

Dona Eis Requiem

When the message first was drafted,
your words were most sincere;
the spontaneity of your kiss
gave meaning to your song.

As birdsong once exalted me,
so too did your words when we met;
they were basis for a rapture never captured
later by pre-meditations or contrivances.

Our love was born in the early morning,
was distorted by evening-time.
We sacrificed our natural rhythm
destroyed our perfect cadences.

Diluted passion failed to penetrate,
restrained by your quest for perfection
in the asymmetrical face
of love and artistic endeavour.

Now moulded by distorted expectation,
bridled by old values and ideals,
we choked on the dust of our dying love,
broken by the breathlessness we feared.

Birth Day

I rode in as if on shore-line waves;
left spinning in the churning waters
mirrored by a cloudless sky,
beyond the reach of men.

Taken down to fathoms, dense
with shingle from an oscillating tide;
me, entangled by gravity's pull,
released to the open sky.

Accurate as the heron's dive;
abandoning all restraint, I flowed
in surrender; these, my agile limbs,
allowing the storm to lead.

I rode in submissive humility, held
in a moment of internal trust,
from the womb to the birthing point,
where my journey was begun.

Mutual Demise

Tell me you're not hurting,
holding your heart at bay;
tell me that your sadness
does not steal your liberty.
Tell me of your musings
when we last embraced,
when the time had come for parting,
unable to deny the truth
that your sorrow fails to hide:
that it still lives on between us;
a truth you've come to know.

I won't dispute our discord
at times before the end;
but for all our diverse thinking,
there's a fire that burns inside.
Tell me it's not happiness
that pervades us as we sit
disinhibited, and talking of our past.
Convince me of your heartfelt wish
to leave our love behind
before you land another blow
that will lead to our mutual demise.

Chameleon

I believe in the night;
honest saviour of the distorted day;
the crest of the hill
as the climb is done.
Here the body sleeps,
immaculately poised
to bestow upon itself,
still, even then, unwaking,
the dream and ease
of its descent to the valley below,
fast and heavy water streaming
where footsteps used to tread
on stones washed clean
in the clarity of dawn.

I believe too in chameleon,
stood in perfection, stock still
upon its rock;
aware of me, he unflinching,
as I, cool and alert,
awash with colour, here transposing,
flatter with impersonation.
I believe in his existence
from those years all past,
when time stood still,
and he grew to the measure
of his changing seasons,

I envy this reptile his night,
its shadow-y home bringing him
light and transmutation
in the still forever hours
while the hornet sleeps.
He stood before me
as a lion upon his throne,
reminding me of my strong mother.
Steadfast, and full of colour,
she took solace in the stars.

Magnificent Day

This is my magnificent day!
I have blessed our house and prayed for rain;
I've laid the tulips upon my father's grave,
and my blessings are all counted.
My bed is loosely made,
that I may sleep tonight with the angels
after my selfless day.

But I can't help but think
of the girl with the curly hair
who reported me for spitting as I spoke.
A wicked nun punished me, 4 years old,
by standing me on a table
and slapping the back of my legs.
She left me crying into my sleeve
as she banished me to the corner
where the dunces go.

And I'll fill my bowl with kindness
just as my mother did
to anoint me with her blessings.
I'll prepare for her return from work
as I stand against the wall
outside the school when school is over
and the kids have all gone home.
I'll hide my shame inside my pants,
firmly crossing my legs as I lean;

afraid to ask if I could be excused.
There I'll remain, glued to the spot,
should I miss her rushing home
round the corner to cook my tea;
or in case she doesn't notice me.

Today is my magnificent day!
I have done my best for others,
and I remember my mother's loving words.

Storm nor Stress

I chased the fulfilment of desire
and left here empty-handed;
there was no trace of substance held,
nor shadow cast upon the road I took.

I thought my whim a tangible thing
for moulding, as though a solid clay;
but my heart had other means to show
the limitation of ideals.

Truth disclosed a detail,
that long evaded me; revealing
insight, strewn beyond the senses,
now held in my sacred heart.

I turned to face a night-long past;
no more is the story told,
for there is nothing left of storm,
nor stress to be a threat.

The Blackbird

The sun at last was less intense.
Laying back in its warm embrace,
I was mesmerized by a blackbird's evening song;
my grasp weakened as I let things go;
clinging no more to old trappings.
I gazed upon lost opportunities to love,
where always I sought to be loved.
Man enough now to see
without regret all that I lost;
instead, I could see through conceit,
deceit and fathomless self-pity.

Song of the blackbird,
ever composed in a moment of spontaneity,
each phrase, a new thought melody never the same,
always to soar, and come to rest in my soul,
I found a moment's clarity
as befits my vacant mind,
taken to heart in the wings of that bird,
and cossetted till my thoughts lie still.
Regaining a moment's reflection,
my lonesome blackbird flew away.

Before the clock struck five, she was gone;
her silence rang through the light breeze.
I leaned back in contentment,
back against the grass that was my bed

for the afternoon.
I rose to the shapes and scents of evening;
a small garden, where holly-hock
and sweet pea were growing fast,
and the rose-bush shed its countless petals
on the earth below.

It will soon be midsummer's day;
but this is the day I'll remember in the evening light.
I'll wait for the blackbird to arrive tomorrow,
to listen once more to her lonesome tones.

Off the Radar

I lost sight of you in the dark.
You're gone from view;
off the radar,
my vision faltering further as I speak.
I thought I caught a glimpse
or heard a murmur from you
as I peered into the murky deep.
Are you perhaps still there
in my walled garden?

I keep the faith I had in you
to return in your radiance
as you always did,
singing like a poet
in your open-hearted way;
spilling your emotion
as you held your dignity close.

But this is not the time
to remember what you were.
Now's the time to ponder,
and resolve the pain that thought inflicts,
without the colour of your response;
without the warmth I've known in you.

Return wild dove to me once more;
rise from the dark corners of my heart;

shed light once more upon
the paths we've yet to tread;
let me know you have kept
your strong hold upon my soul,
my long-lost dove of the night,
child of mother nature.

Warlords

I sit in judgement of the warlord
who threatens the children and their families
with fear and intimidation,
by a hand that eliminates freedom.
I condemn all warlords to an isolated silence,
and carried out in the misery of their gulags.

The very thought of war,
the desolation and torment of it,
the greed of the perpetrators for its furtherance,
their ultimate dissatisfaction,
ever more their greed.

War,
the crazy, wild, extreme hunger for it;
hungry the warlords, addicted to victory,
the pursuit of, the mere love of it
pervading the senses.

Never mind the horror resulting,
futile horror of the loss of lives,
destruction of homes,
scattering families,
the pawns in their game,
held up as trophies
by remembrance parades,
and sanctimonious leaders;

by kings and queens,
and soldiers and their grievers.

Past, Present, Future

If yesterday has taught us valued lessons
that mould us in our efforts to survive,
it's only by discarding our attachment
to the past, we find the freedom now to grow.

As today becomes a puff of clouded vision
when we put aside the future and the past,
it is only at the whim of present moments
that we glimpse the possibility of how.

Though tomorrow works its way into the present,
we contemplate, predict or just suppose;
it's driven here by not much more than hope
or wish-fulfilment in the thought that shapes desire.

Pete wrote this for me, I'm blessed.

My Hero, Ellie

Ellie
xxx

You are my hero;
the model I cannot emulate.
Knowing you has broken my defences
and moved my mountains;
you have watered my valleys
so that rivers run wild:
wild and free to reflect
your wild, free soul.

I love you more than love,
deeper than the mighty rivers
that flow in the face of death.
I follow your river to my sea.

Though I hide my light,
yet still your fire burns brightly.
No shadow; nor flickering; but lasting
beyond your life and your senses.
You are the loved one; no matter what you do.

But you deserve much more
than these mere niceties.
You deserve it all: love in the extreme
to offset all you give.
Your power penetrates my meagre sympathies;
reduces my vanity to this solitary tear
I shed for you alone.

Ode to Poetry

Cradle to grave you hold me.
You carry the weight and the flame;
you corner my demons in their infancy
as they limp to an early grave.

Whenever a voice from within me calls,
you form a shape for me of its essence.
to wear as persona or a song.

Your message runs through me like fire
or meekly as melancholy can often be,
with words not born of thought nor reason,
though their song rebounds
with the echo of my unbending truth.

I may have held my tongue when young,
but old, I have no shame;
no lack of self-respect can hold me to account.

You give me worth,
usher me through darkness,
offer explanations
for what at first I misconstrue.

You speak for me
and call me out whenever I'm not true;
you lift me from dark waters;

you take me as I am,
and give me room to fly.

Homecoming

Housed here,
memory littered with moments gone and put aside;
unremembered detail fading still further,
leaving more than a glimpse of what it meant
to be a thousand miles away, only yesterday.

Lost to all that,
as I lie in my cloaked world
my soul, my only company,
I journey to the sound of oceans new,
hardly knowing, neither guessing
nor even awaiting
the next grief that will unfold.

Back here,
re-rooted with my trees,
following the scent of new flowers,
roses in back rooms and lobbies, tidy like nature,
awash with life and colour in the corners of my eyes,
a thousand possibilities waiting
for my focus to fall upon them,
exciting their waves to flow as tears
that will surround my heart and cleanse my sorrow.

I have become as father to a child,
showing them the path and pointing the way
before returning home; to be housed here

where all has grown more simple and serene,
where memory lives out its dying wish . . .
that my rest will be sublime,
and my eternal spirit will rise once more.

Cotton Sheets

Awoke to find
you were gone from mind;
arose to prepare my way;
washed my hands and face of you,
all trace of you,
and all that went before.

But when your cotton sheets
at last had come to mind,
my heart cried out so loud before
the old obsession awoke
and crept back in.
Those were times
so tough, but now they've gone.

I still lie in cotton sheets at times;
all through the night.
I awake to find you gone from mind
but I sleep alone again.

Perhaps

Perhaps it will arrive after I'm gone,
the ultimate ecstasy;
fear of death behind us;
life untampered with;
senses dangling in a cloudless sky.

Or perhaps it will be tomorrow,
before the sun
that scorches the skin of those left
living out a dream;
discarding their reality.

Perhaps it will be short and sweet,
like the death of me;
life's memories crumbling
in the hands of fate,
void of sound, not even voice.

Or perhaps it will shake
the rafters of my tomb;
vision gone forever,
insight turned to dust,
desire lying on a stone-cold floor.

Perhaps I've been a fool all along,
as I lie here before the end;
this life reminding me that all

has been a dream, inauthentic, false,
all but a delusion, perhaps.

Unknown Depths (for Tristan)

Beyond the walls
of senses lie
the unknown depths
of an unknown world;
a blank canvas
awaits its fate,
words are set
in concrete, just
before the pen
is drawn.

The skin contracts
in icy waters,
the chattering tongue
retracts its vows.
Silence pervades
the early morning field,
as two of us stroll
to the water's edge.

The father in me
slips into the last
days of creation.
The son holds out
his strong hand
to haul me up

to the pleasant peace
of a new morning.

Essence

If I am doing nothing,
eyes lowered to the floor,
taking in shapes
without naming them,
just to look,
not to see, nor to describe;
and if I hear, not listen,
just hear and not describe;
without explaining,
it all becomes just being,
true essence of what I am.
If I feel my body;
sense it there,
neither moving
nor a part of it,
I feel without feeling,
then there is nothing,
nothing, that sacred something,
deep inside,
true essence of what I am.

Solo

Solo, I cannot be equal;
I converse with others,
confronted by our differences;
I am ever unequal,
separate in my solitude.

I have let what I see
fade to nothing;
when thoughts arise,
I allow them to cascade.

Alone in time with the silence,
my memory stuck inside a dream;
there's not a thing
I can do to re-arrange it;
my heart beats to an old familiar theme.

Love No More

I heard her say before the breeze
'it won't be long till breath no more
will pass between these lips of ours
so lately here, so soon to close'.

I heard her whisper from afar,
'sad to be alone once more',
while I, in chilly evening air,
brought forth a sigh to quell my fear.

Her gentle voice would hardly sound
above the storm so soon to rage
from night till morning as I mourned,
after she had left me there.

She stirred, as if to turn around
to help me heal a broken wing,
uprooted as our love was now,
and left to fade in one fell swoop.

I felt her pass behind me, slow,
as when the the night descends upon
the ravages of long fought battles,
while I, the warrior, walked on alone.

And then at once as day-break dawned,
I saw the years before me, bleak,

as if I never would behold her face
again, nor stroke her scented hair.

I saw her after love's defeat,
gliding through the crowd in haste
without so much as a passing glance
nor flick of hair; then she was gone.

Gone as are those times of old
when she would think the best of me,
before the leaves began to fall,
before she whispered 'love no more'.

Only This

I often dreamed of heaven;
long craved the clarity
of space between the thoughts.
But a stranger to the truth,
I spoke in metaphors
before the metal effigies
of an old master.
All to no avail.
Ideas would gush unleashed,
confuse and nullify the mind.

But now I breathe clear-mindedness;
it lives on, ever expanding
between the thoughts invading.
Nothing comes and goes.
I am the truth;
that ever living truth
around my heart.
I am awareness,
nothing more, nothing less.
Not a thing, nor no-thing,
I am consciousness,
in the empty-ing of the mind,
in the spaciousness of no mind.

Tanker

Though once I wept, I weep no more;
tomorrow came defiantly,
barging past my boundary
like a tanker through a narrow canal.

Bearing nerves of steel I'd strut
across those bridges burning for me,
breaking down resistant strains
of all my former melancholy.

Without so much a whisper, I'll
declare whatever comes to me
in thought or rapt emotion
with a passion from the soul.

You will not see the weeping lad
nor floundering lost child in me;
you'll only see my gliding ship unswayed
by the wildest waters of my sea.

D.H.E.

Way beyond the torment of your years,
I look for you in corners of my memory,
resigned to facing mysteries you left.
You took roads I never dreamed of
since those days behind the curtain where you hid.
I walked with you, still in my youth unknowing
how your hand would guide me
on the road I chose.
Tell me where did all that music lead you,
convoluted rhythms making sense
of all the madness of those times?
Though I was slow to learn, I never left you;
In fact I'm still here looking for you, see?
I talk to what is left of you remembered,
wondering what is left of you to hear.
The edges of your paintings they may curl
and your colours will at last begin to fade.
But I'm spectator left in your vast arena,
your precious cargo sitting in my distant warehouse
with those who picked you up along the way.
I may not see you now, but still I hear you.
And I will take you with me to my grave.

Three for Crysse

1

If I could break a silence
for a minute, whilst you're still here,
I have to let you know
that when I speak of love,
or stroke your hand that doesn't stir
it's a love that's known
only to those of us
whose paths
your heart has touched
in the bright corridors
you have walked.

2

You were in pain,
with your white face still smiling,
your small body seeking its rest
against the pillows behind you.
Woman of clarity,
loved by so many, I but one,
my tears had to wait til I drove away.
You said it was not the best of days.
I fumbled around
not knowing what to say
and you did what you do,
making it easy for me;
asking of my plans for the day,
both of us avoiding the fact
that this was the last time we'd meet.
I told you how much you mean to me;
you told me you'll remember me forever.

3

Are you gone sweet woman?
I thought I heard your voice.
Are you somewhere in the ether,
or some other place I don't know?

Fond farewells and accolades,
from all of those who love you,
have pushed your journey onwards,
endless poetry in every line.

I held you more closely, clearly,
in your last few months on earth;
you surpassed all expectations.
I could never once have guessed.

Now and Then

Before, I wrote in riddles
on a page torn from my past:
thoughts from a sleeping mind.
   Now, I breathe the air of the forest,
   create no more such desperate lines.

Once, I slept in doorways,
with the wind around my head;
lost within the nightmare of a past.
   Now, I wake with senses all departed,
   and no desire to sing such sad refrains.

Then was all I had to do
to break through clouds of sorrow
to forge a way to this my home in mind.
   Here and now, discarded like the wind,
   no longer is there need for that despair.

For Lizzi

I walked into your world today,
leaving mine behind;
the steps I took were simple
though I brought
our old attachments along:
joy, happiness, sorrow and pain.

I live across two worlds now
with no more bridges to cross;
whichever one appears,
I find eternity in my love for you,
transcending the impossible
and bringing forth
our own personal truth.

Where?

Where have the days gone,
soft and early;
days we knew
and loved so fairly?
I was never born for this,
the era of neglected bliss.

Bliss for me this silence brewing
in the warmth of lovers wooing,
when simple ruled as simple was,
thought discarded, just because.

Oblivious

My life is a lonely thing.
I take it out from time to time,
into the mist of self-doubt,
to search amongst
the fields of memory
for reasons, or for ecstasy.

It wanders through these ruins
in pursuit of understanding;
but I walk on alone,
oblivious to my own confusion.

Each to the Other

How fragile is the universe,
how brash and yet so sad.
It brings upon itself the pain
and violence of woman and man,
each to the other.

Alone I wander,
decade to the next,
to seek a universal
strength of purpose;
just a moment's respite
when all our hearts
are beating in time,
each to the other.

Serene of face, extending the hand,
a welcome in the moment
by all who, gathered here,
have set all law aside in their humility,
to be as one with,
each to the other.

Untold Mystery

I lost today
the most secret of all my secrets:
my own integrity;
given away unknowingly
in a moment of need
to be more than what I am.

Self-contained now,
spread out upon the land,
exposed for all to see;
with not so much a whisper of regret
I live on, with lost parts gone
that once were one,
though ravaged further on
by the storms of untold mystery.

You in the Mirror

Who are you?
You in the mirror. Yes you!
I don't recognise you anymore.
You used to love looking back
at me, your creator, your *alter ego*.
Now you look tired and sad.
Of course, I never knew you fully.
Only what you showed me.
I didn't see you really.
Only what I wanted.
I created you in my own image;
you rewarded me
with your armour on;
that I never saw beyond.
You were not true to me;
nor I to you.
I deceived you into living
beyond your own reality.
Your response was to deceive me
into believing in you.
You, who was never really real to me!
Just an image in the mirror
that I nurtured
at the expense of my own truth.

So who are you, old man?
Show me again who you are,

that I may learn of your reality;
to accept you as you are.
And if I co-erced you
into believing
what you see before you,
I ask you to forgive,
so that I may accept you
as the reflection that you are,
and not an image
I have come to believe
is the truth of what I am.

Milton Keynes UK
Ingram Content Group UK Ltd.
UKHW051139200923
429021UK00010B/93